M Charlene Stutzman

W9-DHX-711

Valentine's Day
THINGS TO MAKE AND DO

Written by Robyn Supraner
Illustrated by Renzo Barto

Troll Associates

Library of Congress Cataloging in Publication Data

Supraner, Robyn.
 Valentine's Day.

 SUMMARY: Instructions for making decorations, book-
marks, jewelry, and other crafts for Valentine's Day.
 1. Valentine decorations—Juvenile literature.
2. Handicraft—Juvenile literature. [1. Valentine
decorations. 2. Handicraft] I. Barto, Renzo.
II. Title.
TT900.V34S96   745.594'1   80-23780
ISBN 0-89375-424-2
ISBN 0-89375-425-0 (pbk.)

Copyright © 1981 by Troll Associates, Mahwah, New Jersey.
All rights reserved. No part of this book may be used or
reproduced in any manner whatsoever without written permission
from the publisher. Printed in the United States of America.
10 9 8 7 6 5 4 3 2 1

CONTENTS

Before You Begin   4

Making a Valentine Heart   6

Valentine Collage   8

Happy Valentine's Day Banner   10

Bookmark   12

A Giant Valentine Fold-Out Card   16

Kooky Clay   18

Hearts and Flowers Necklace   20

Silhouettes   24

Pomander Ball   28

Stained-Glass Hearts   30

Valentine Checkers   32

Valentine Checkerboard   34

Hearty Potato Prints   36

Gift Cards   38

Tissue-Paper Bouquet   40

Hearts and Flowers Mobile   44

This Is Your Life!   46

Before you begin—

Read all the directions.

Have everything you need ready.

Spread old newspapers on the table, when you are using paint or glue.

Save your scraps; they may come in handy.

Leave time enough to clean up when you are finished.

Valentine's Day is a time to say, "I like you," or "I love you," or "I think you're very nice." So take your time. Have patience. But most of all, have fun!

MAKING A VALENTINE HEART

Valentine's Day wouldn't be Valentine's Day without lots and lots of hearts. Here's how to make them in all shapes and sizes.

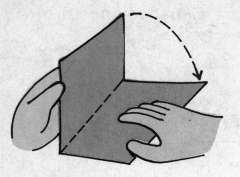

1 Fold a piece of paper.

2 Draw half a heart on it.

3 Cut it out carefully.

4 When you open the paper, you will have a perfect heart!

5 Here are patterns for skinny hearts, fat hearts, and regular hearts. You will want to use them all.

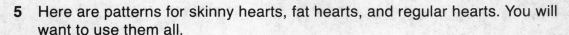
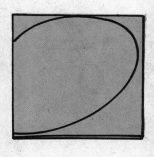
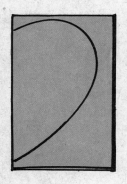

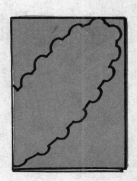

Practice cutting both smooth-edged and curly-edged hearts. After a while, you will be able to make them without using a pattern.

VALENTINE COLLAGE

Here's what you need:

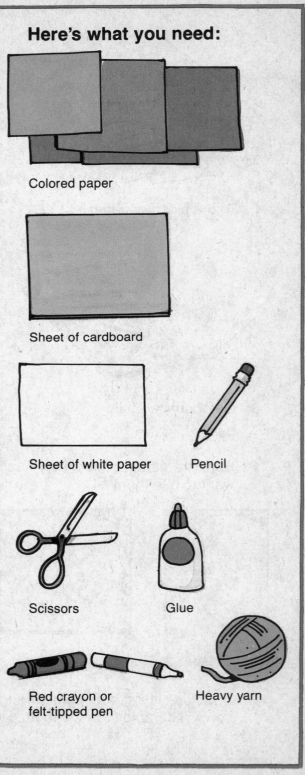

Colored paper

Sheet of cardboard

Sheet of white paper

Pencil

Scissors

Glue

Red crayon or
felt-tipped pen

Heavy yarn

Here's what you do:

1 Make a large heart. Trace it on a sheet of cardboard. Cut out the cardboard heart.

2 Cut lots and lots of hearts from colored paper. Make them different sizes and colors.

3 Glue them to the cardboard heart. Overlap the hearts so every bit of cardboard is covered.

4 Make enough small red hearts to go around the border. Make them the same size. Glue them in place.

5 Cut a small rectangle from

a piece of white paper. Draw a red border around it. Glue it to the heart. This is a place for you to write a valentine message.

6 Glue the ends of a piece of heavy yarn to the back of the collage to make a loop.

Use your collage as a decoration or hang it around the neck of someone you love!

HAPPY VALENTINE'S DAY BANNER

Here's what you need:

Ruler

Colored construction paper

Heavy, white typing paper

Pencil

Scissors

Glue

Cellophane tape

Here's what you do:

1 Cut 18, 3 × 6-inch rectangles out of colored construction paper.

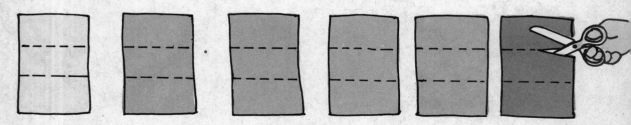

(*Note:* A half sheet of 9 × 12 paper will give you 3 rectangles.)

Make 3 yellow rectangles, 3 pink, 3 green, 3 light blue, 3 dark blue, and 3 orange. Don't worry if you don't have all the colors. Use whatever colors you have.

2 Cut a letter from each rectangle.

3 Cut 2 hearts from 2 4½-inch squares of red construction paper. Then make a small, skinny heart for the apostrophe.

4 Join 7 sheets of white paper with cellophane tape. This is the banner.

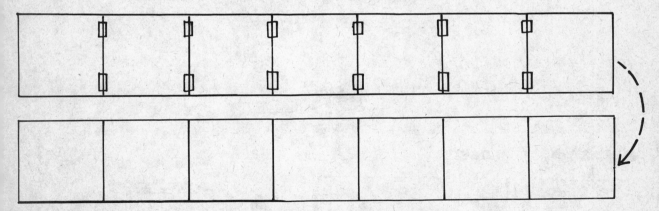

5 Turn the banner over. Glue the letters and hearts in place.

6 Add more white paper, if you need it.

BOOKMARK

Here's what you need:

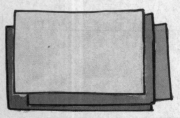

Colored construction paper

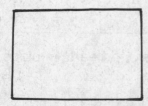

Oak tag or cardboard

Glue

Pencil

Black marker

Scissors

17

KOOKY CLAY

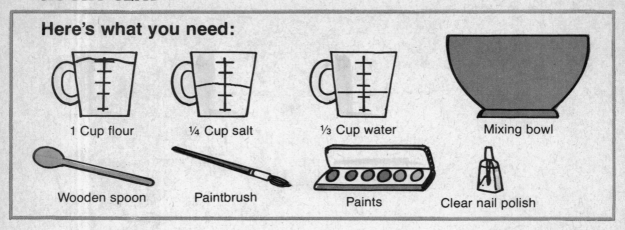

Here's what you need:

1 Cup flour   ¼ Cup salt   ⅓ Cup water   Mixing bowl

Wooden spoon   Paintbrush   Paints   Clear nail polish

Here's what you do:

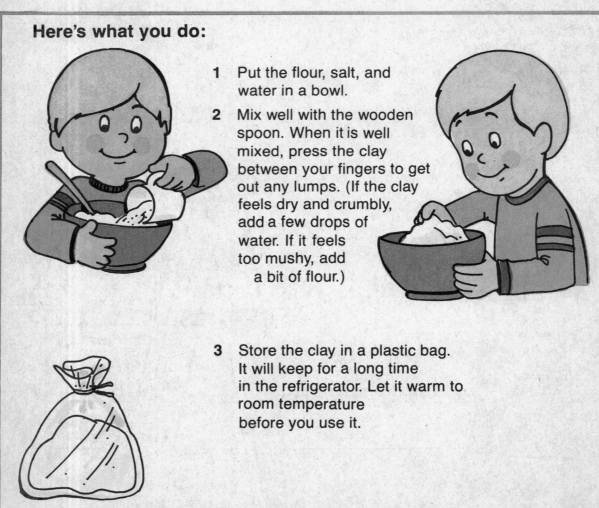

1 Put the flour, salt, and water in a bowl.

2 Mix well with the wooden spoon. When it is well mixed, press the clay between your fingers to get out any lumps. (If the clay feels dry and crumbly, add a few drops of water. If it feels too mushy, add a bit of flour.)

3 Store the clay in a plastic bag. It will keep for a long time in the refrigerator. Let it warm to room temperature before you use it.

Kooky Clay is good for making small figures. They can be painted with any water-base paint. You can give the painted clay a nice shine by brushing on a coat of clear nail polish. Here are a few ideas for figures you can make—or design your own!

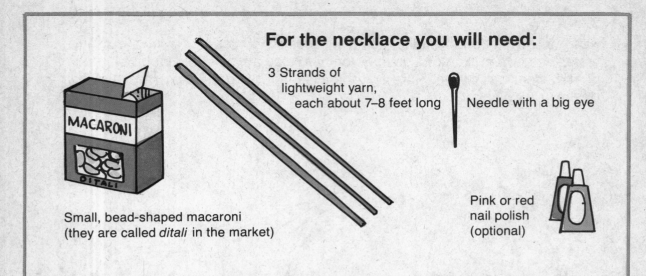

For the necklace you will need:

3 Strands of
lightweight yarn,
each about 7–8 feet long

Needle with a big eye

MACARONI

DITALI

Small, bead-shaped macaroni
(they are called *ditali* in the market)

Pink or red
nail polish
(optional)

Here's what you do:

1 Knot together 3 strands of yarn. Leave a 6-inch tassle at one end. Thread the needle at other end.
(*Note:* If you like, color the macaroni with pink or red nail polish. Be sure it is dry before threading it.)

2 Thread the yarn through a piece of macaroni.

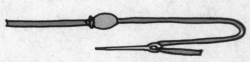

3 Tie a second knot close to the macaroni.

4 Continue threading macaroni and knotting the yarn until you are about 7 inches from the end. Finish with a knot. Leave another 6-inch tassle.

5 Knot the tassles together.

HEARTS
AND FLOWERS
NECKLACE

For the heart and the flower you will need:

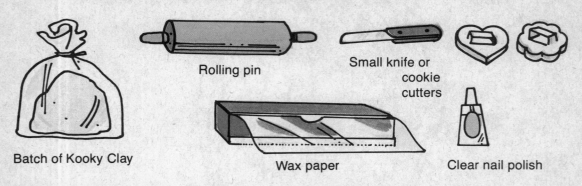

Batch of Kooky Clay

Rolling pin

Small knife or cookie cutters

Wax paper

Clear nail polish

Here's what you do:

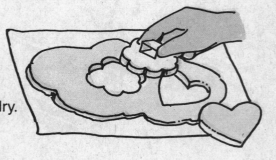

1 On a sheet of wax paper, roll out the clay to ¼-inch thick.

2 With a small knife or cookie cutters, cut out a heart and a flower. Poke a hole in each for stringing. Put them aside for 2 or 3 days, until they are dry.

3 Color the flower and the heart with the red and pink nail polish you used for the macaroni.

4 When they are dry, brush them with a coat of clear polish.

5 Tie the heart and flower to the necklace with the strand of yarn from each tassle.

SILHOUETTES

You will need help with part of this project. Share the work with a friend. Afterwards, you can exchange silhouettes.

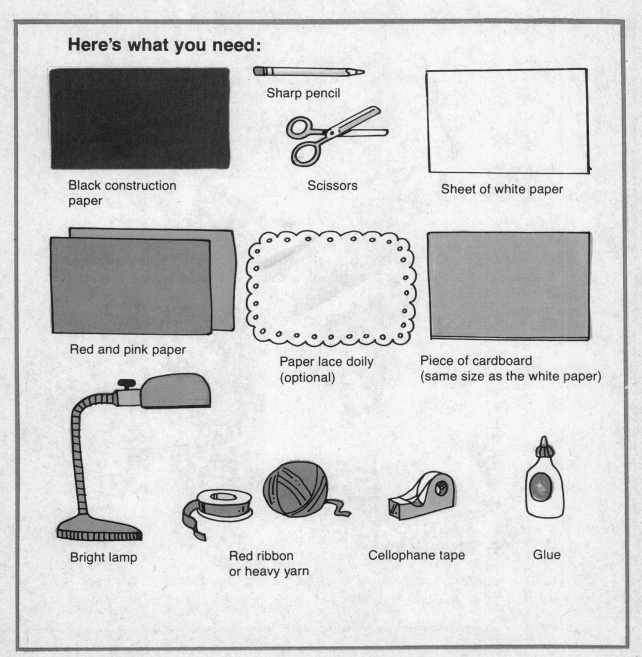

Here's what you need:

Black construction paper

Sharp pencil

Scissors

Sheet of white paper

Red and pink paper

Paper lace doily (optional)

Piece of cardboard (same size as the white paper)

Bright lamp

Red ribbon or heavy yarn

Cellophane tape

Glue

Here's what you do:

1 Stand between a bright light and an empty wall. Stand sideways so the shadow of your profile falls on the wall. Use a bright lamp or pick a sunny day when the sun casts a strong shadow.

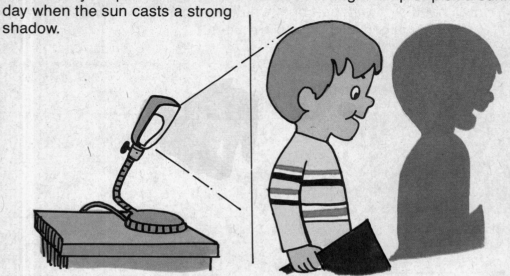

2 Tape a sheet of black construction paper against the wall, so your shadow falls on the paper. If the light is bright, it will cast a shadow, even on black paper. The shadow is a silhouette.

3 Ask someone to trace your silhouette on the paper. Remember to stand very still! Now, you can finish the rest by yourself.

4 Very carefully, cut out the silhouette and set it aside.

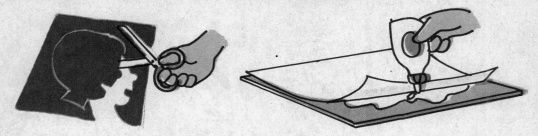

5 Glue a sheet of white paper to a piece of cardboard. Place the silhouette in the center and glue it in place.

6 Cut out hearts from the pink construction paper, and cut smaller hearts from the red construction paper.

7 Decorate the border of the white paper with pink hearts. Glue a small, red heart on each pink heart. If you really want to be fancy, add a bit of paper lace from a doily.

8 Tape red ribbon or heavy yarn to the back of the silhouette. Hang it from a hook or use a bulletin board tack. A silhouette makes an especially nice valentine gift. Do you know someone who would like one?

POMANDER BALL

Here's what you need:

An orange

Box of
whole cloves

Sprinkle of
cinnamon

Sprinkle of
nutmeg

Pretty yarn
or ribbon

Here's what you do:

1 Stick the stems of the cloves into an orange. Put them as close together as you can. Cover the whole orange.

2 Sprinkle the orange with cinnamon and nutmeg.

3 Tie the pomander ball in a ribbon. Make a loop for hanging the ball. Add a pretty bow.

4 Put it in a box with tissue paper, and give it as a gift. You can make a pomander ball with an apple, too.

Hang the pomander ball in your closet or tuck it in a drawer. Everything will smell fresh and spicy!

STAINED-GLASS HEARTS

Here's what you need:

Black construction
paper

Colored sheets
of cellophane

Cellophane
tape

White pencil

Scissors

Glue and brush
(optional)

Here's what you do:

1 Copy this pattern for stained-glass hearts on black construction paper or make a pattern of your own.

2 Carefully, cut out the parts that are to be colored.

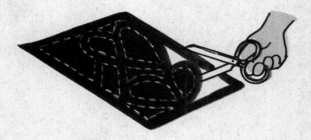

3 Tape different colored cellophane to the back of the paper.

(*Note:* Blue cellophane over yellow will give you green. Red over yellow will give you orange. Red over blue will give you purple.)

4 If you like, brush a bit of glue across the cellophane. It will look more like glass. Tape your stained-glass hearts to a sunny window.

VALENTINE CHECKERS

Here's what you need:

Double batch of Kooky Clay

Sheet of wax paper

Small, heart-shaped cookie cutter

Paint set and brush

Clear nail polish (optional)

Paper towels

Rolling pin

Here's what you do:

1 Divide the Kooky Clay
into 2 balls.
Cover 1 ball with a damp paper towel until you are ready to use it.

2 Roll out the other ball on a sheet
of wax paper. The clay should be
about ¼-inch thick.

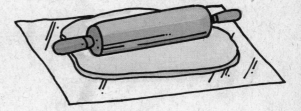

3 Using a cookie cutter, cut out 12 small hearts. Set them aside.

4 Do the same thing with the second ball of clay.

5 Place the hearts on a sheet of wax paper, and let them dry for 2 or 3 days.

6 Paint 12 hearts pink. Paint 12 hearts red.

7 When they are dry, they will look bright and shiny if you brush a coat of clear
nail polish on each heart.

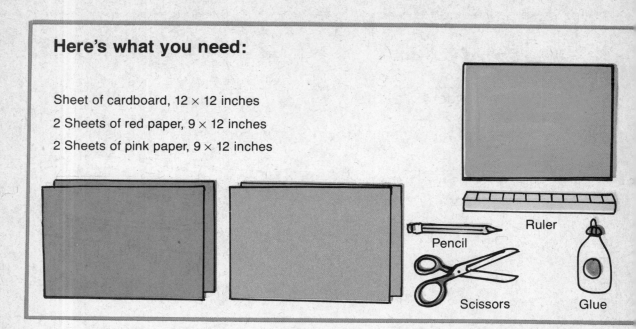

Here's what you need:

Sheet of cardboard, 12 × 12 inches

2 Sheets of red paper, 9 × 12 inches

2 Sheets of pink paper, 9 × 12 inches

Pencil

Ruler

Scissors

Glue

VALENTINE CHECKERBOARD

Here's what you do:

1   Cut 8 strips from the red paper. Each strip should be 1½ × 12 inches.

2   Cut 8 strips of the same size from the pink paper.

3   Glue 2 red strips and 2 pink strips at the corners where they overlap to form a 12-inch square. Place them as shown in the top drawing.

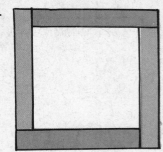

4   Place the 6 remaining red strips across the square, as shown in the middle drawing. Glue the ends of each strip to the square.

5   Weave the 6 pink strips in and out through the red strips to form a checkerboard.

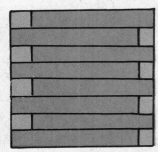

6   Put glue on one side of the cardboard, and press checkerboard against glue.

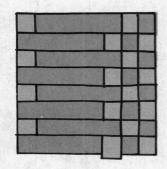

With your valentine checkers and checkerboard, you're ready for a game of checkers with someone you like!

HEARTY POTATO PRINTS

Here's what you need:

Tissue or shelving paper

Potato

Pencil

Small knife

Poster paints and paintbrush

Here's what you do:

1 Wash and dry a potato.

2 Cut it in half.

3 Draw a pattern on the cut surface of half the potato. Draw another pattern on the other half. Keep the patterns simple. A big heart and a small heart are good. A heart and an arrow are good, too.

4 With a knife, cut away any potato that is not part of the pattern. After you do this, the shape you are going to print will be raised from the rest of the potato.

5 Cover the raised part with a light coat of poster paint.

6 Lightly press the potato on a sheet of tissue or shelving paper. When the pattern fades, paint the potato again.

7 Print your patterns in different designs. Try a border of hearts and arrows. Try an all-over design of big and little hearts. Let one color dry, then print over it with another color. Experiment. You will discover many beautiful designs. Use the finished paper to wrap a special gift. You also can use potato prints to decorate valentine cards.

GIFT CARDS

This is a good way to use those scraps of paper you've been saving.

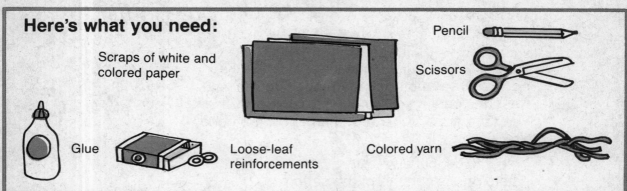

Here's what you need:

Scraps of white and colored paper

Pencil

Scissors

Glue

Loose-leaf reinforcements

Colored yarn

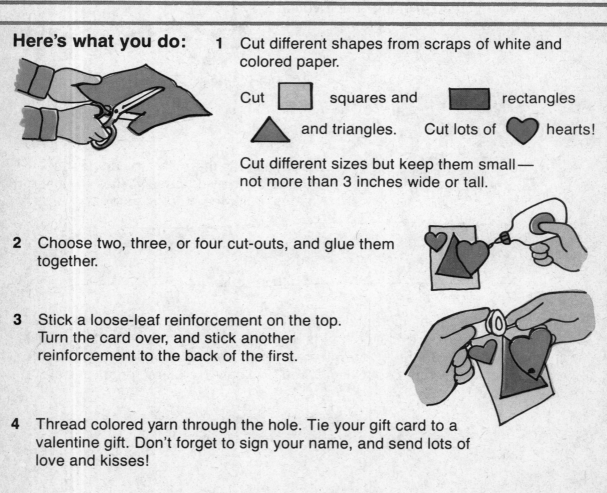

Here's what you do:

1 Cut different shapes from scraps of white and colored paper.

Cut [ ] squares and [ ] rectangles and triangles. Cut lots of ♥ hearts!

Cut different sizes but keep them small— not more than 3 inches wide or tall.

2 Choose two, three, or four cut-outs, and glue them together.

3 Stick a loose-leaf reinforcement on the top. Turn the card over, and stick another reinforcement to the back of the first.

4 Thread colored yarn through the hole. Tie your gift card to a valentine gift. Don't forget to sign your name, and send lots of love and kisses!

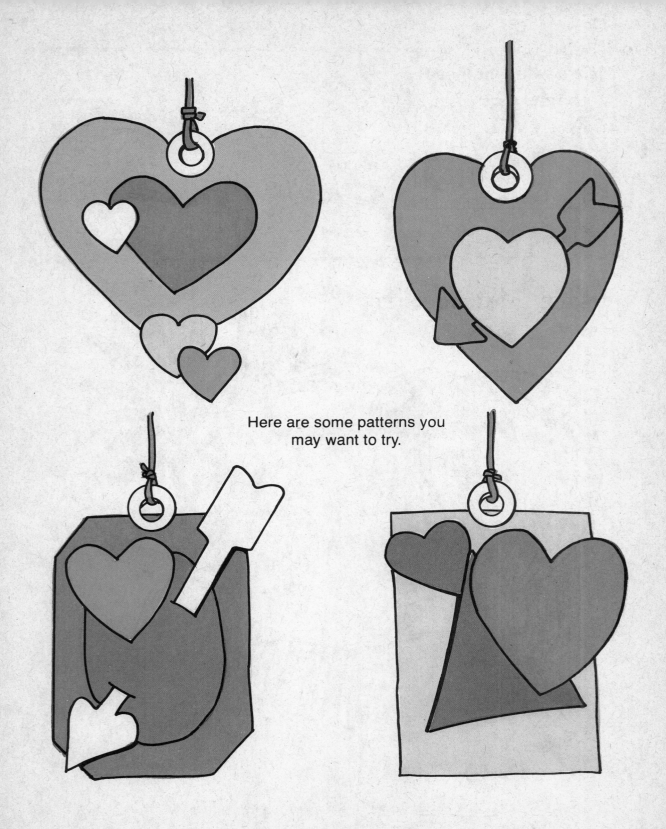

Here are some patterns you
may want to try.

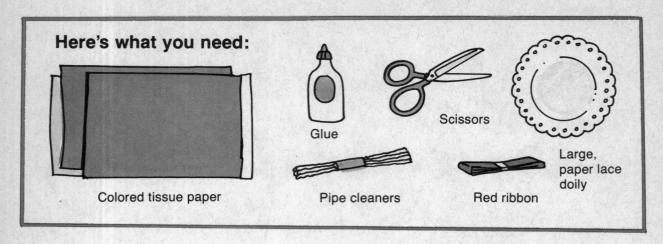

Here's what you need:

Colored tissue paper

Glue

Scissors

Pipe cleaners

Red ribbon

Large, paper lace doily

TISSUE-PAPER BOUQUET

Here's what you do:

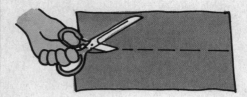

1 Cut a 4-inch-wide strip from a piece of violet-colored tissue paper.

2 Fold the strip in half. Fold it in half again ... and again ... and again.

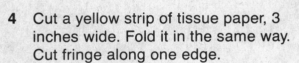

3 Cut the paper in the shape shown in the drawing. These will be the petals of your flower.

4 Cut a yellow strip of tissue paper, 3 inches wide. Fold it in the same way. Cut fringe along one edge.

5 Wrap the strip of yellow tissue around a pipe cleaner. Hold it in place with a drop of glue.

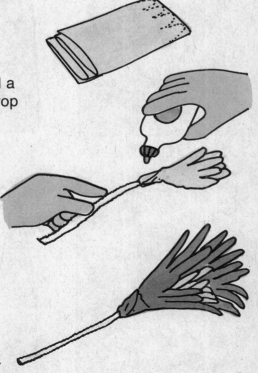

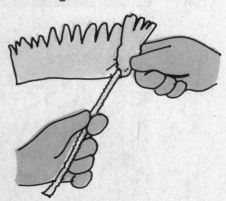

6 Wrap the strip of violet tissue paper around the yellow paper. Use another bit of glue to hold it in place.

7 Cut a long strip of green tissue paper, 2 inches wide. Wrap the bottom of the flower and the pipe cleaner with the green tissue. Glue it in place.

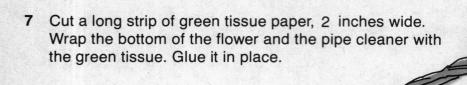

8 Here are some other shapes you can use for petals and centers. Make flowers with petals of more than one color. Make some flowers with tall centers and short petals. Use your imagination to combine shapes and colors in different ways.

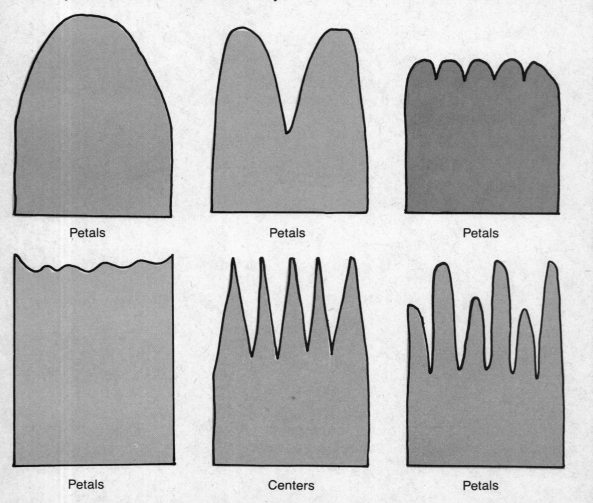

Petals   Petals   Petals

Petals   Centers   Petals

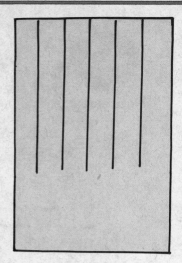

Centers

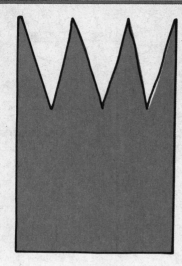

Petals

9 Fold the paper lace doily gently in half. Do not make a sharp crease. Fold it in half again.

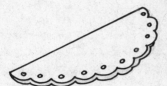

10 Snip off the tip of the folded doily. Open the doily and you will have a small hole in the center.

11 Fit the stems of the flowers through the hole.

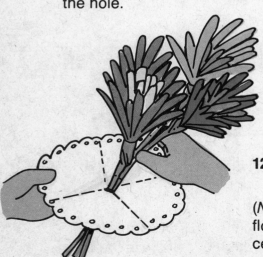

12 Gather the doily and tie it with red ribbon.

(*Note:* Try reversing the way you make the flowers. Use petals for the centers, and use centers for the petals.)

HEARTS AND FLOWERS MOBILE

Here's what you need:

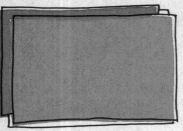

Pink, red, and white construction paper

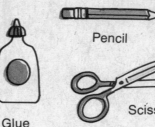

Glue

Pencil

Scissors

Piece of yarn, about 3½ feet long

Straws

Here's what you do:

1 Fold two, 3 x 9-inch strips of red construction paper like an accordion. Each small rectangle should be 1½ x 3 inches.

2 Cut half of a heart shape in the folded paper. Glue the open ends of the heart together. Place a length of yarn through the center of the hearts. Glue the yarn in place.

3 From a 4 x 10-inch strip of pink construction paper, cut out a triangle shape from each end. Fold and glue the two ends, as shown in the drawing.

4 Make three small holes in the strip of paper, one in the center and one at each end. This is the banner of the mobile.

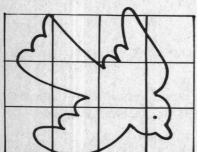

5 Cut two dove shapes out of white construction paper. Glue the birds to the two ends of the banner.

6 Take three, 6-inch lengths of yarn—one piece of yarn goes through each hole in the banner.

7 Fold two, 3 x 6-inch pieces of white construction paper. Cut out a flower shape. From red construction paper, cut out four, 1-inch circles. Glue each red circle to the center of each flower. Place a 6-inch length of yarn through each flower. Glue the sides of the flowers together, with the yarn held in the middle.

8 Make three holes in each straw

as shown in the drawing. Thread the yarn at each end of the banner through the center hole of each straw and knot the yarn. At the holes in the ends of each straw, thread a heart and a flower; knot the yarn.

9 Print the name of a special friend on the banner. The mobile is ready to be hung in the air where it will slowly move and turn.

THIS IS YOUR LIFE!

This is something very special to make for someone very dear.

Here's what you need:

Magazines with colored pictures

Scissors   Glue

Sheet of heavy white cardboard

Decorations: paper lace doily, ribbon, colored paper, and whatever else you think is pretty.

Here's what you do:

1   Look through the magazines. Cut out anything that reminds you of the person for whom you are making this gift. If the person loves basketball, look for pictures of basketball players. Try to find pictures of your friend's favorite foods. If it's music he or she likes, look for musical instruments. Use a scrap of sheet music. Find a picture of a hi-fi and some records. Include as many of the person's interests as you can. Use photographs. Cut out letters. Arrange them to spell a poem or message about your friend.

2 Glue everything on a sheet of heavy white cardboard. Arrange it all to look as nice as you can. Add a few gold stars and a bunch of hearts! Or use a bit of lace. Remember everything special about that person and find the pictures to say it all. When you are finished, you will have made a truly special gift!